BEWARE OF THE
STEAM ROLLER
WILLIAM LAMBERT HORSMONDEN

STEAM ROLLERS IN FOCUS

by John Crawley

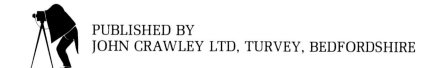

PUBLISHED BY
JOHN CRAWLEY LTD, TURVEY, BEDFORDSHIRE

©JOHN CRAWLEY LTD 1986

First published in 1986 by
John Crawley Limited
Field House, Turvey
Bedfordshire MK43 8DU

Printed in Great Britain by
AB Printers Limited, Leicester

ISBN 0 9508046 4 9

The endpapers show William Lambert, the well
known steam rolling contractor of Horsmonden,
Kent posing in front of an early Aveling & Porter
single cylinder convertible steam roller with men of
his road gang.

To my mother
Dorothy Crawley
who's tolerance and
enthusiasm engendered
my love of steam.

FOREWORD

by Ronald Adams
Director and General Manager
Eddison Plant Hire

Some forty years ago, I started my working life with steam rollers: now the invitation to write the foreword to this book gives me a most welcome opportunity to relive those years through its pages.

In 1943, I was apprenticed to the Eddison Steam Rolling Company of Dorchester, and was given the customary first job of making water-lifter nozzles. I could never have imagined, as I progressed through the trade, that my last job in steam would be to dispose of the fleet in the south west of England.

It was a painful task to give the order to scrap these impressive products of individual skill and craftsmanship, and I was greatly pleased to be able to sell to enthusiasts a dozen or so of the rollers at £25-£30 each, knowing that they would be saved to fascinate future generations.

They were certainly built to last: a roller which slid off an embankment, for instance, and landed upside down, would present terrible problems in those days when large mobile cranes were unknown; but, once righted and back on the road after maybe days of jacking and packing, the roller could be at work again after only one more day.

This robust machinery is also visually impressive: the rotating flywheel, the valve gear, can all be seen doing their job, unlike the enclosed parts of the internal combustion engine. It isn't surprising that modern heavy plant doesn't seem to attract the same tolerance, and affection, as the old steam rollers did, even when their plumes of smoke signalled delays to holiday traffic in the narrow west country lanes.

I congratulate John Crawley for preserving and publishing these delightful photographs. For me personally it was a joy to see them and savour the memories they revived; taking a broader view, the pictures collected here are not only a record of our industrial heritage and the history of our road system, but also of a whole way of life.

In those days, a driver might spend most of his working life with one engine, which would be known to the firm by the name he had given it, and regarded as almost his own property; whole families (with the local authorities turning a blind eye to the regulations) even lived with all their goods, and the pet dog, in the roller vans, in a way that for good or ill, would scarcely be allowed today.

Though the winds of change have blown all that away, it is still within living memory, and I am very glad to see this book appear in time to capture first-hand the authentic history of an era from the people who made it.

Ronald Adams
April 1986

BEWARE
OF
STEAMROLLERS

INTRODUCTION

Without doubt the most popular of all steam road engines is the steam roller. Commercially they outlived all the other types and by the nature of their work were very much in the public eye.

By the time they were cast aside the preservation movement had got underway so when offered for sale many made prices far higher than the scrap man was willing to pay: numerous examples have therefore been saved, with most makes being represented. Aveling & Porter Ltd of Rochester made more steam rollers than all the other makers put together which accounts for the profusion of photographs of their products.

For the benefit of my younger readers let me digress for a moment and set the scene in the 1930s.

A horse and cart would proceed along the road in a series of stops and starts while a man shovelled out gravel to make heaps on the pavement every few yards; from another horse and cart a workman would unload and place in position a wooden gate like structure, occupying nearly half the width of the road, on the top plank of which were painted the words **BEWARE OF STEAM ROLLER**, whilst on the end, stuck in a socket at an angle, was a red flag; from the cart other men unloaded shovels and brushes and then set about sweeping the road's surface to rid it of loose stones and dust.

As soon as a good length of road had been so treated the horse drawn tar baby, a tar tank on wheels with a chimney and a fire underneath to keep the tar liquid, would slowly move up the swept portion of the road whilst its attendant workman would deposit pools of tar on the road for the other men, wearing heavy tar encrusted boots, to brush over the surface and into all the cracks and crannies.

When a section had been completed the next job was to spread the gravel from the heaps on the pavement, which the men did in a kind of sweeping turn. A last flick as the gravel was about to leave the shovel made sure it landed just where it was required, leaving no bald patches of tar.

By now the steam roller had arrived and stood quietly waiting to do its share of the work once the men had progressed far enough up the road. The driver would busy himself with an oil can, throw a few shovelfuls of coal onto the fire, then with a pulling and pushing of levers (which I now realise was the means of engaging the low speed gear for rolling) he was ready. A tap on the regulator and then the magic moment, a gentle chuff, chuff, chuff, the smell of coal smoke, the grating crunch of gravel on steel rolls, the smell of sweet cylinder oil mingled with the scent of hot tar...this to a small boy was what it was all about, a scenario which once experienced lives for ever.

Enough of the nostalgia and back to this volume. As in my earlier books, machines in preservation are marked ■ after the engine number, and the building date given is usually that on which the engine became available to the sales department for collection or delivery.

To the many contributors of photographs, which are all individually acknowledged, I offer my sincere thanks; to David Phillips of the University of Reading Institute of Agricultural History and English Rural Life, and to Alan Duke for his continuing support in helping to solve the many queries that arose during the compilation of this book.

I must also thank the Road Roller Association, an organisation formed in 1974 to bring together all those who have an interest in both steam and motor rollers.

If, after reading this volume you feel that you would like to join them, just send me a stamped addressed envelope and I will see that you receive details of the Association. You don't have to own a roller, but I cannot promise that this will remain the case! It is a very absorbing interest.

John Crawley

LIST OF PLATES

Engine No.	Plate	Page
William Allchin & Co Ltd		
Globe Works, Northampton		
1131 ■	1	9
1131 ■	2	9
1187 ■	3	10
1187 ■	4	10
Sir W.G. Armstrong, Whitworth & Co Ltd		
Openshaw, Manchester		
8R2	5	11
8R12	6	11
8R19	7	12
8R22	8	12
10R17 ■	9	13
10R22 ■	10	13
10R22 ■	11	14
10R22 ■	12	14
10R30	13	14
10R32	14	15
10R32	15	15
10R32	16	15
10R35 ■	17	16
10R36	18	16
10R50 ■	19	17
10R50 ■	20	17
10R50 ■	21	17
Tandem, no details	22	18
Tandem, no details	23	18
Aveling-Barford Ltd		
Grantham, Lincolnshire		
AD387	24	19
No details	25	19
Aveling & Porter Ltd		
Rochester, Kent		
500	26	20
607	27	20
608	28	21
806	29	21
882	30	22
1814	31	22
1829	32	23
2020	33	23
2323	34	24
2324	35	24
2510	36	25
2862	37	25
3101	38	25
3101	39	26
3316	40	26
3523	41	26
3616	42	27
3864	43	27
4004	44	27
4111	45	28
4214 ■	46	28
4505 ■	47	29
4749	48	29
4800	49	29
4800	50	30
4907	51	30
4919	52	30
4988	53	31
5028	54	31
5138	55	31
5406	56	32
5662	57	32
5905	58	32
6165 ■	59	33
6378 ■	60	33
6538	61	33
6676	62	34
6745	63	34
7071	64	34
No details	65	35
No details	66	35
7411 ■	67	36
7411 ■	68	36
7411 ■	69	36
7411 ■	70	37
No details	71	38
No details	72	38
No details	73	39
No details	74	39
7828	75	40
9078	76	40
9155 ■	77	40
9186	78	41
9192	79	41
9216	80	41
9399	81	42
10058	82	42
10072 ■	83	42
10159 ■	84	43
10235 ■	77	40
10245	85	43
10258	86	44
10410	87	44
10410	88	44
10421	89	45
10444	90	45
10555 ■	91	46
10828	92	46
10926 ■	93	46
10939	94	47
10998	95	47
11671	96	47
12156 ■	97	48
No details	98	48
14113 ■	99	49
No details	100	49
Charles Burrell & Sons Ltd		
St Nicholas Works, Thetford, Norfolk		
2145	101	50
2338	102	50
2535	103	51
2717	104	51
2769	105	52
3047 ■	106	52
3150	107	53
3150	108	53
3301	109	54
3301	110	54
3313 ■	111	55

Engine No.	Plate	Page
3313 ■	112	55
3359	113	56
3359	114	56
3364	115	57
3760	116	57
3760	117	57
3946 ■	118	58
4002	119	58
4005 ■	120	59
4022	121	59
4047	122	60
4052	123	60
4058 ■	124	61
4058 ■	125	61
No details	126	62
4083 ■	127	62

Clayton & Shuttleworth Ltd
Lincoln

Engine No.	Plate	Page
35350	128	63
44279	129	63
48751 ■	130	64
48792	131	64
49003	132	64

Clayton Wagons Ltd
Titanic Works, Lincoln

Engine No.	Plate	Page
T1090	133	65

William Foster & Company Ltd
Wellington Foundry, Lincoln

Engine No.	Plate	Page
13088 ■	134	65

John Fowler & Company (Leeds) Ltd
Steam Plough Works, Leeds, Yorkshire

Engine No.	Plate	Page
4614	135	66
4839	136	66
6475	137	67
6754	138	67
7943	139	68
Bomford Scarifier	140	68
8593	141	69
9008	142	69
9147	143	70
9299	144	70
9852	145	71
9852	146	72
10105	147	72
10155	148	72
10156	149	73
10808	150	73
13457	151	74
13457	152	74
15589 ■	153	75
15589 ■	154	75
15942 ■	155	76
Invincible Scarifier	156	76
16096	157	77
16096	158	77
16096	159	77
16272	160	78
16272	161	79
16615 ■	162	79

Engine No.	Plate	Page
18070 ■	163	80
21833 ■	164	80

Richard Garrett & Sons Ltd
Leiston, Suffolk

Engine No.	Plate	Page
21411	165	81
27163	166	81
33636 ■	167	82
34084 ■	168	82
34085	169	83
34267 ■	170	83
34267 ■	171	84
34267 ■	172	84
34267 ■	173	85
34706 ■	174	85

Thomas Green & Son Ltd
Smithfield Ironworks, Leeds, Yorkshire

Engine No.	Plate	Page
No detail	175	86
1374	176	86
1430	177	87
1505	178	87
1508 ■	179	88
1508 ■	180	88
1666	181	89
No details	182	89
1976	183	90
1995	184	90
2007 ■	185	91
2201	186	91
2408	187	92
No details	188	92

J. & H. McLaren Ltd
Midland Engine Works, Leeds, Yorkshire

Engine No.	Plate	Page
284	189	93
284	190	93
1694	191	94
1694	192	94
1694	193	95
1702	194	95

Manning Wardle & Company
Boyne Engine Works, Leeds, Yorkshire

Engine No.	Plate	Page
No details	195	96
No details	196	96

**Manns Patent Steam Cart
& Wagon Company**
Hunslet, Leeds, Yorkshire

Engine No.	Plate	Page
No details	197	97
No details	198	97

Marshall Sons & Co Ltd
Gainsborough, Lincolnshire

Engine No.	Plate	Page
40047 ■	199	98
72096 ■	200	98
73821	201	99
76634	202	99
76945	203	100
Tandem, no details	204	100
Tandem, no details	205	101
Tandem, no details	206	101

Engine No.	Plate	Page
Tandem, no details	207	101
78667 ■	208	102
78928	209	102
78953 ■	210	103
79087 ■	211	103
80224 ■ (79444)	212	104
80224 ■ (79444)	213	104
80730	214	105
84620 ■	215	105
86990	216	106
86990	217	106
87125 ■	218	107
87635 ■	219	107

Ransomes, Sims & Jefferies Ltd
Ipswich, Suffolk

Engine No.	Plate	Page
11829	220	107

Robey & Co Ltd
Globe Works, Lincoln

Engine No.	Plate	Page
40651	221	108
41609	222	108
42156	223	109
44083 ■	224	109
44083 ■	225	109
46935 ■	226	110
48869 ■	227	110

Ruston, Proctor & Co Ltd
Sheaf Iron Works, Lincoln

Engine No.	Plate	Page
26620	228	111
No details	229	111
No details	230	112
43831	231	112
43833	232	113

Ruston & Hornsby Ltd
Sheaf Iron Works, Lincoln

Engine No.	Plate	Page
52785 ■	233	113
112562	234	114
157574	235	114
157574	236	114

W. Tasker & Sons Ltd
Waterloo Iron Works, Andover, Hampshire

Engine No.	Plate	Page
1715 ■	237	115
1913	238	115

Wallis & Steevens Ltd
Hampshire Iron Works, Basingstoke, Hants

Engine No.	Plate	Page
No details	239	116
2539	240	116
2556	241	116
2572	242	117
2813	243	117
2816	244	118
2889	245	118
2978	246	118
7070	247	119
7128	248	119
7234	249	120
7715	250	120
7723	251	120
7737	252	121
7772	253	121
7776	254	121
7785	255	122
7797	256	122
7799 ■	257	122
7832 ■	258	123
7837	259	123
7863 ■	260	124
7878 ■	261	124
7884 ■	262	125
7903	263	125
7937	264	126
7937	265	126
7947 ■	266	127
7948 ■	267	127
7962 ■	268	128
8030 ■	269	128
8050	270	128

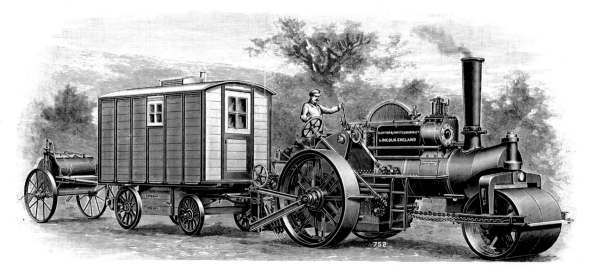

1 & 2.   Allchin 10 ton single cylinder steam roller No 1131 ■, Registration No NH 3416, was built in February 1900, the first steam roller to be built by William Allchin Ltd of Globe Works, Northampton. She was sold to the Northampton Corporation where she became No 1 in their fleet and is now preserved in their ownership.

Left: Allchin No 1131 ■ photographed on 14th July 1951 in St James Depot, Northampton.
(courtesy P.N. Williams)

Below: Allchin No 1131 ■ undergoing repair in St James Depot, Northampton (date unknown).
(courtesy G. Alliez)

3 & 4. Allchin 10 ton single cylinder steam roller No 1187 ■, Registration No NH 8417 was built in November 1901 and sold to Northampton Corporation where she became No 2 in their fleet and spent her working life. In January 1961 she was sold into preservation. These two photographs show 1187 ■ at work in Greville Avenue, Spinney Hill, Northampton on 19th July 1959.

(courtesy G.H. Starmer)

5. Armstrong Whitworth 8 ton compound steam roller No 8R2, Registration No AX 5417, was built in September 1923, but, strangely, existing records fail to record the owners of this machine. The photograph shows her at work at Blaenavon, Monmouthshire in 1952.   *(courtesy F. Jones)*

6. Armstrong Whitworth 8 ton compound steam roller No 8R12, Registration No ND 7367, was built in August 1924 and retained by the makers for use in their hire fleet. She was later sold to John Allen & Sons Ltd, Oxford and became No 130 in their fleet. By July 1951 she was in the ownership of A.E. Hatton of Sutton-in-Ashfield where she was last licenced in December 1956. She was finally scrapped by B.A. Mitchell of Shirebrook, Derby. This photograph was taken at Mansfield in June 1954. *(courtesy F. Jones)*

7.   Armstrong Whitworth 8 ton compound steam roller No 8R19, Registration No NE 1780, was built in 1925 and sold to John Allen & Sons (Oxford) Ltd where she became No 133 in their fleet, spending her working life with this company.   *(courtesy C. Roads)*

8.   Armstrong Whitworth 8 ton compound steam roller No 8R22, Registration No PF 4113, was built in August 1926 and sold to Caterham Urban District Council, Surrey. In October 1954 she was sold to C.W. Lambert of Horsmonden, Kent, who resold her the following year to M. Lynch & Sons of Rochester, Kent. Later that same year they sold her for scrap to H.J. & R. Saunders Co Ltd of Leytonstone, in whose yard she is seen in June 1956.   *(courtesy F. Jones)*

9.   Armstrong Whitworth 10 ton compound steam roller No 10R17 ■, Registration No CA 7184, was built in October 1924 and sold to Wrexham Rural District Council, later being acquired by Denbighshire County Council. She spent the rest of her working life with the County Council before being sold into preservation in 1963. Photographed at Ruthin, Denbighshire in June 1960.   *(courtesy F. Jones)*

10.   Armstrong Whitworth 10 ton compound steam roller No 10R22 ■, Registration No DX 4602, was built in September 1924 and sold to the Ipswich Dock Commissioners where she spent her working life before being sold into preservation. This photograph was taken on New Cut West, Ipswich, on 5th March 1936.

(courtesy R.G. Pratt)

11. Armstrong Whitworth No 10R22 ■ on New Cut West at Ipswich on the 5th March 1936.
(courtesy R.G. Pratt)

12. Armstrong Whitworth No 10R22 ■ at Cliff Quarry, Ipswich in 1938.
(courtesy W.P. Riley/B.D. Stoyel)

13. Armstrong Whitworth 10 ton compound steam roller No 10R30, Registration No AF 9725, was built in 1924 and sold to Falmouth Corporation, Cornwall. She spent all her working life with the Corporation and was recorded as being for sale in 1963. This photograph was taken at the Trecectman Road Depot, Falmouth, in December 1953.
(courtesy P. Tambling)

14. Armstrong Whitworth
10 ton compound steam roller
No 10R32, Registration No
NE 2294, was built in 1925 and
retained by the makers for use
in their hire fleet. She was
later sold to Bodles Ltd of
Bexhill, East Sussex, the first
of a succession of owners; by
1935 French Bros of Seaford,
East Sussex; by 1936
C.W. Lambert of Horsmonden,
Kent; 1937 William Hooker of
Langley, Kent; 1946 A. Savage
of Bexhill; 1949 Hatch of
Pembury, Kent and finally T.
Hughson Ltd of Bexhill-on-Sea
where she was eventually
scrapped in 1955. On the
evidence of this constant
change of ownership it would
appear that this example, at
least, did not come up to the
owners' expectations. This
photograph shows her on trade
plates, but no date is recorded.
(courtesy R.G. Pratt)

15.   Armstrong Whitworth
No 10R32 whilst in the
ownership of William Hooker
of Langley, Kent.
(courtesy P. Love)

16.   Armstrong Whitworth
No 10R32 at Newenden on
29th August 1954 in the
ownership of Hughson Ltd, by
now the scarifier had been
removed and a canopy fitted.
(courtesy B.D. Stoyel)

17.   Armstrong Whitworth 10 ton compound steam roller No 10R35 ■, Registration No NE 2271, was built in June 1925 and eventually sold to John Allen & Sons (Oxford) Ltd. In 1948 she was purchased by Hughson Ltd of Hawkhurst, Kent. Photographed on 6th June 1958 shortly after being sold into preservation.

(courtesy W.S. Love)

18.   Armstrong Whitworth 10 ton compound steam roller No 10R36, Registration No NE 2119, was built in 1925 and retained by the makers for use in their hire fleet. In 1931 she was sold to the Lancashire Road Rolling Company, she became No 110 in their fleet and spent the rest of her working life with this owner. Shown at work in New Road, Salterforth on 10th July 1934.

(courtesy W.P. Riley/B.D. Stoyel)

19, 20 & 21.   Armstrong Whitworth 10ton compound steam roller No 10R50 ■, Registration No NF 4098, was built in 1927 and retained by the makers for use in their hire fleet. She was bought by Samuel Jackson Sons Ltd of Wistaston, who sold her eventually to W.E. Gale & Sons of Whittlesey. These three photographs show the roller at work at Wisbech, Cambridge-shire, in August 1954.
(courtesy Ronald H. Clark)

22 & 23.   Armstrong Whitworth 8 ton Type QR (Quick Reverse) steam roller fitted with duplex cylinders was built circa 1929, received Registration No BA 9263, and sold to Wilson & Wilkinson Ltd of Salford, Lancashire where she spent her working life, surviving to the late 1950s. Designed for rolling asphalt carpeting this type had many commendable design features with the boiler firebox and side tanks being fitted to a chassis frame, but the front roll mounted beneath the boiler increased their overall height and made them very unstable to operate, even on the most moderately cambered roads. These two photographs show the Type QR roller working at Burnley in August 1953.   *(courtesy W.P. Riley/B.D. Stoyel)*

24.   Aveling Barford 10 ton Type 'T' single cylinder steam roller No AD387 was built in November 1939 and sold to the Executive Engineer, City Division, Public Works Department, Calcutta, India, where she is seen working in this photograph. *(courtesy Aveling Barford Ltd)*

25.   Aveling Barford Type 'GS' prototype steam roller was built in 1947, based on the GD8 14 ton post-World War Two series roller. The company had received an enquiry for diesel and steam rollers, the former to work in coastal areas where oil was available, the steamer in the interior, sharing as many common parts as possible in order to keep the range of spare parts stocked to a minimum. The design was based on the GD8 14 ton post-World War Two series. Probably on the grounds of price the customer eventually settled for GD diesels and conventional steam rollers, so the GS never progressed beyond the prototype seen here under test at Grantham in December 1947. *(courtesy Aveling Barford Ltd)*

26. Aveling & Porter 15 ton single cylinder steam roller No 500 (works number 13, indicating the thirteenth steam roller), was built in June 1869 but the name of her prospective owner was deleted from the works records. In February 1872 she was sold to Mowlem Freeman & Company, London.

(courtesy Institute of Agricultural History)

27. Aveling & Porter 15 ton single cylinder steam roller No 607 was built in November 1870 and sold to the vestry of St George, Hanover Square, London. *(courtesy Ronald H. Clark)*

28.   Aveling & Porter 15 ton single cylinder steam roller No 608, Registration No AT 5789, was built in November 1870 and sold to the Hull Local Board where she became No 1 in their fleet and where she spent all of her working life, being last licenced in 1924.   *(author's collection)*

29.   Aveling & Porter 15 ton single cylinder steam roller No 806 was built in 1872 and exported to Melbourne, Australia. This was the first steam roller to be sent out to Australia and the 49th production machine built at Rochester.   *(courtesy Aveling-Barford Ltd)*

30. Aveling & Porter 15 ton single cylinder steam roller thought to be No 882 was built in November 1872 and sold to John Mowlem & Company, Blackheath, London.

(courtesy Ronald H. Clark)

31. Aveling & Porter 10 ton single cylinder steam roller No 1814, Registration No KK 2840, was built in December 1882 and sold to Thomas Wood & Sons Ltd of Crockenhill, Kent where she spent the next 50 years before being cut up in 1933. Cotton reel steering gear is fitted to this roller where the steering chains are attached to the ends of the cross shaft rather than in the centre which became the normal practice. This photograph, taken at Tonbridge circa 1904, shows Mr John Carter of the Tonbridge Council by the front roll.

(courtesy Thomas Wood & Sons Ltd)

32.   Aveling & Porter 10 ton single cylinder steam roller No 1829, Registration No KK 2839, was built in January 1883 and sold to Thomas Wood & Sons Ltd of Crockenhill, Kent, where she remained all of her working life. This photograph was taken circa 1920 and shows driver George Gilham Jnr, with George Gilham senior by the scarifier. In 1932 she was involved in a road accident finishing up in the foyer of the New Cross Cinema and was scrapped some two years later.   *(courtesy Thomas Wood & Sons Ltd)*

33.   Aveling & Porter 15 ton single cylinder steam roller No 2020 was built in January 1885 and sold to Maidstone Local Board. In 1921 she was sold to W.W. Buncombe of Highbridge, Somerset where she became No 27 in their fleet and worked until 1931. The date of this photograph is not known but shows her at work in Exeter for the Exeter Corporation with their Council Foreman and Driver Duffey.   *(courtesy N.D. Buncombe)*

34.   Aveling & Porter 22 ton double cylinder steam roller No 2323 was built in November 1887 to an order by Findlay, Durham & Brodie, the London purchasing agents for the Kimberley diamond fields in South Africa. She was used for crushing blue stone when searching for diamonds and was fitted with a wrought iron harrow with 28 steel tines for loosening the rolled blue stone.   *(courtesy Ronald H. Clark)*

35.   Aveling & Porter 10 ton single cylinder steam roller No 2324 was built in November 1887 and sold to Thomas Wood of Crockenhill, Kent being No 8 in their fleet. She spent all of her working life with Woods until cut up in 1904. This photograph was taken in their yard circa 1902 and shows Master Thomas Henry Wood at the regulator, Thomas Raymond Wood in the coal bunker with their works manager Walter Gilham standing by the rear roll.   *(courtesy Thomas Wood & Sons Ltd)*

36. Aveling & Porter (centre) 10 ton single cylinder steam roller No 2510 was built in July 1889 and sold to Hornsey Local Board, London. By November 1904 she had been sold to Eddison Steam Rolling Company of Dorchester where she became No 137 in their fleet, later receiving the Registration No FX 6956. In this photograph she is seen with two other Aveling & Porter steam rollers (numbers unknown) providing dead weight for a deflection test on Ballingdon Bridge, Sudbury, Suffolk, circa 1911.
(courtesy R.G. Pratt)

37. Aveling & Porter 10 ton single cylinder steam roller No 2862 was built in July 1891 and sold to Tipton Local Board, Staffordshire. By 1928 she had been sold to Jeremiah Carley of Chatteris, Ely where she received the Registration No EB 7458. She was later sold to Herbert T. Gentle of Stotfold, Bedfordshire where she received the Registration No MJ 6047 and her last recorded owner was P.C. Kidman & Sons of Biggleswade.
(courtesy C. Roads)

38. Aveling & Porter 10 ton single cylinder steam roller No 3101 was built in October 1892 and sold to Blackheath Highways Board, London. She was sold to Hambledon Rural District Council, Surrey where she received the Registration No YA 1555 and in 1913 she was acquired by W.E. Buncombe of Highbridge, Somerset where she became their Fleet No 19. This photograph, taken in Highbridge Council yard prior to working in the town, shows left to right: Jim Bond; Sidney Buncombe; Gaffer Woodward, Foreman Highbridge Urban District Council; Arthur Elliott, fitter; and E.W. Buncombe; the driver's name is not recorded.
(courtesy N.D. Buncombe)

39.   Another photograph of Aveling & Porter No 3101 taken in the mid-twenties in the New Forest, Hampshire, with driver Bliss and his wife and child who lived and travelled with him in the living van behind the roller. By this time the roller had been fitted with an awning.

(courtesy N.D. Buncombe)

40.   Aveling & Porter 10 ton single cylinder steam roller No 3316 was built in December 1893 and sold to F.A. Jackson & Co of Finsbury Park, London. She was later acquired by Charles H. Abrahams of Holloway, London. Her last recorded owners were T. Cowman & Son of Ashfordby where she became No 7 in their fleet and acquired the Registration No NR 16. This photograph shows her whilst at work in the ownership of F. Cowman & Son.

(courtesy G.R. Hawthorne)

41.   Aveling & Porter 10 ton compound steam roller No 3523, Registration No TB 2712, was built in March 1895 and sold to the Earl of Derby at Knowsley, Lancashire. At an unrecorded date she was sold to W.C. Sutton & Sons of Beckermet, Cumberland, to whom she belonged at the time of this accident when the edge of the road gave way and she slid into the ditch. The wire ropes are attached to the winch of a traction engine just out of view on the right of this photograph.

(author's collection)

42. Aveling & Porter 15 ton compound steam roller No 3616, Registration No TB 8166 was built in October 1895 and sold to Chorley Corporation Lancashire. Later she was sold to Isaac Ball & Sons of Wharles, Lancashire where she became their Fleet No 6 and where she spent the rest of her working life.
(courtesy W.P. Riley/B.D. Stoyel)

43. Aveling & Porter 10 ton single cylinder steam roller No 3864, Registration No L 8965, was built in February 1897 and sold to Llandaff & Dinas Powys Rural District Council and later became No 2 in the fleet belonging to Cardiff Rural District Council. She finished her working life in the ownership of R.E. Palmer of Great Massingham, Norfolk.
(courtesy G.R. Hawthorne)

44. Aveling & Porter 10 ton single cylinder steam roller No 4004, Registration No PC 9226, was built in November 1897 and sold to A.J. Ward & Sons of Egham, Surrey, where she spent her working life. This photograph was taken at Colnbrook on 9th May 1952.
(courtesy R.E. Tustin)

45.   Aveling & Porter 10 ton compound steam roller No 4111, Registration No FR 2865, was built in May 1898 and sold to Blackpool Corporation where she became No 3 in their fleet. By 1924 she had been sold to A.M. Cole of Sleaford, Lincs, where she worked for six years before being sold to her last owners W. & J. Morfoot of Shipdham, Norfolk. At the time this photograph was taken in 1928 near Heckington when working for Sleaford Rural District Council with her driver Jim Proctor, she was still carrying the brass number 3 on her headstock from her Blackpool days.

(courtesy J. Proctor)

46.   Aveling & Porter 12½ ton single cylinder steam roller No 4214 ■ was built in October 1898 and sold to John Knight of Daybrook, Nottinghamshire. In July 1921 she was sold to W.W. Buncombe of Highbridge, Somerset where she became their Fleet No 48. This photograph was taken circa 1904 at Carlton, Nottinghamshire and shows her at work rolling tarmacadam; her owner/driver, John Knight, is on the left.

(courtesy N.D. Buncombe)

47. Aveling & Porter 10 ton single cylinder steam roller No 4505 ■ was built in March 1900 and sold to Christchurch Rural District Council in Hampshire. In 1910 she was taken back by the makers, presumably in part exchange as she was sold later the same year to Bomford & Evershed of Salford Priors. By February 1919 she was in the ownership of W.C. Sutton & Sons of Beckermet, Cumberland where she received the Registration No AO 8101. In 1958 she was acquired by H.F. Smith & Son of Hexham, Northumberland and was finally sold into preservation in 1965. This photograph was taken at Distington, Cumberland in August 1953.

(courtesy R.G. Pratt)

48. Aveling & Porter convertible steam roller No 4749, Registration No NM 615, was built in July 1901 and sold to Bedford Corporation where she spent all of her working life. This photograph was taken in Bromham Road, Bedford in 1938.

(courtesy R.G. Pratt)

49. Aveling & Porter 12½ ton compound steam roller No 4800, Registration No HD 1574, was built in August 1901 and exhibited at the Bradford Show in the same year. She was sold to Hampshire Brothers of Ravensthorpe, Yorkshire, where she spent her working life. This early 1900's photograph shows Joseph Hampshire on the left.

(courtesy J. Hampshire)

50. Aveling & Porter 12½ ton compound steam roller No 4800, Registration No HD 1574, was built in August 1901, exhibited at the Bradford Show in that year and sold to Hampshire Bros of Ravensthorpe, Yorkshire. This photograph was taken in the early 1900s when the roller was on hire to a local council and shows driver Willie Lockwood on the left with one of the original Hampshire brothers next to him.
(courtesy J. Hampshire)

51. Aveling & Porter 10 ton single cylinder steam roller No 4907, Registration No FX 6929, was built in November 1901 and sold to the Eddison Steam Rolling Company of Dorchester, Fleet No 98, where she spent all her working life.
(courtesy Eddison Plant Ltd)

52. Aveling & Porter 10 ton single cylinder steam roller No 4919, Registration No FX6931, was built in December 1901 and sold to the Eddison Steam Rolling Company of Dorchester where she received the Fleet No 100. She spent all her working life with this company.
(courtesy Eddison Plant Ltd)

53. Aveling & Porter 10 ton single cylinder steam roller No 4988, Registration No FX 6938, was built in March 1902 and sold to Eddison Steam Rolling Company of Dorchester where she became No 111 in their fleet. In 1922 she was sold to Friern Barnet UDC, Middlesex. By 1929 she had been sold to Thomas Rowley of Tottenham, London who sold her in 1959 to W. & J. Glossop Ltd of Hipperholme, Yorkshire where she was scrapped in 1964. This photograph shows her at Mitcham, London on 1st October 1950.
(courtesy J.H. Meredith)

54. Aveling & Porter 10 ton single cylinder steam roller No 5028 was built in June 1902 and sold to William Lea of Northleach, Gloucestershire. She was later acquired by Hubert Blackwell, also of Northleach, where she received the Registration No DF 7285. Her next owner was W.W. Buncombe of Highbridge, Somerset, where she became 138 in their fleet. She was last licenced in 1935. This photograph taken in 1932 when owned by W.W. Buncombe shows (left to right): driver Jimmy Towning, Harry Eddington (driver of second engine) and three of Somerset County Council's men whilst working at Bayford Hill, Wincanton. At this time the drivers were receiving £2.50 each per week as wages and the council men 4p per hour.
(courtesy N.D. Buncombe)

55. Aveling & Porter 6 ton single cylinder steam roller No 5138 was built in December 1902 and sold to Tuff & Miskin of Rochester, Kent. Then followed a succession of owners, and with Sutton Coldfield Corporation she received Registration No WD 3282. Her last owner was Joshua Rodgers of South Crosland in the West Riding of Yorkshire, where she was last licenced in 1952. The sloping cylinder was necessary to enable the flywheel, which was mounted on the crankshaft between the hornplates, to clear the firebox crown. This photograph was taken at South Crosland, near Huddersfield.
(courtesy J.A. Smith)

56. Aveling & Porter 4 ton single cylinder tandem roller No 5406, was built in November 1903 and sold to His Grace the Duke of Bedford at Woburn, Bedfordshire. In August 1904 she was sold to the Lancashire Road Rolling Company where she became No 7 in their fleet and was later acquired by Bituminous Surfacing Ltd, Manchester where she spent the rest of her working life. This photograph was taken at Liverpool on 26th August 1945.

(courtesy M.C. Fayers)

57. Aveling & Porter 10 ton single cylinder steam roller No 5662, Registration No FX 6960, was built in January 1905 and sold to Eddison Steam Rolling Company of Dorchester, where she became No 143 in their fleet. In the twenties she was sold to the Liverpool Corporation finally finishing up with Todd Bros (St Helens) Ltd. This photograph was taken on 11th September 1911 at Talgarth in Breconshire by the local photographer W. Howard.

(courtesy Eddison Plant Ltd)

58. Aveling & Porter 10 ton single cylinder steam roller No 5905 was built in December 1905 and sold to the Eddison Steam Rolling Company of Dorchester where she spent all of her working life being No 156 in their fleet. This photograph was taken at Builth Wells after being driven off the railway wagon which had delivered the brand new roller to driver Truman and his mate Dodge. The name on the cylinder lagging, 'Truman's Pride of Wales' and the Fleet No 156 were cut out of paper and stuck on by Truman for the benefit of the photographer. Truman was a vain and unpopular man who, years later, was to stand trial for murder.

(courtesy Eddison Plant Ltd)

59. Aveling & Porter 10 ton compound steam roller No 6165 ■, Registration No MD 4411, was built in January 1907 and sold to Harrow Urban District Council, Middlesex. In 1924 she was sold to W.W. Buncombe of Highbridge, Somerset where she became No 90 in their fleet. This photograph was taken on 14th May 1961, whilst working on the construction of the Bristol Outer Ring Road.

(courtesy N.D. Buncombe)

60. Aveling & Porter 10 ton compound steam roller No 6378 ■, Registration No PB 9581, was built in September 1907 and sold to Kingston-upon-Thames Corporation. In April 1933 she was returned to Aveling & Porter Ltd presumably in part exchange. By 1935 she had been sold to Wm Pye & Son of Lidsing, Chatham, Kent. This photograph was taken on 25th April 1951 at Phoenix Wharf, Stroud.

(courtesy J.H. Meredith)

61. Aveling & Porter 12 ton compound steam roller No 6538, Registration No SA 4190, was built in June 1908 and sold to Aberdeenshire County Council (Deeside District) where she spent all of her working life being No 2 in their fleet. This photograph was taken at work in Ballater in August 1951.

(courtesy J.H. Meredith)

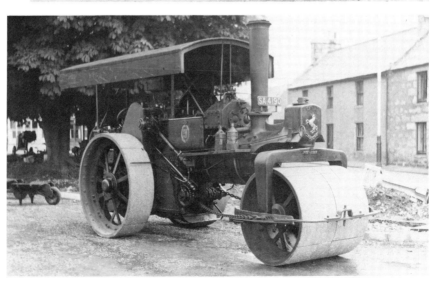

62.   Aveling & Porter 10 ton single cylinder steam roller No 6676, Registration No HR 4410, was built in November 1908 and sold to Mrs Sarah Barnes (Wiltshire Steam Rolling Company) of Southwick, where she spent her working life. This photograph shows her at work in Radlett, Hertfordshire in the 1930s.

(courtesy Ronald H. Clark)

63.   Aveling & Porter 12½ ton single cylinder steam roller No 6745, Registration No NO 2699, was built in March 1909 and sold to Colchester Corporation where she became their Fleet No 2. She spent all of her working life at Colchester where this photograph was taken on 24th January 1936.

(courtesy R.G. Pratt)

64.   Aveling & Porter 10 ton single cylinder steam roller No 7071, was built in May 1910 and sold to Hampshire Bros of Ravensthorpe, Yorkshire. By 1921 she had been sold to Consett Urban District Council in County Durham where she received the Registration No J 6638. It is recorded that she was always a bad engine to make steam.

(courtesy J. Hampshire)

65 & 66.   An Aveling & Porter compound steam roller belonging to Mr Chambers of Clifford, near Hay-on-Wye, Herefordshire. These photographs, circa 1909, show her in a ditch after getting out of control near Kinnersley on the road between Hereford and Hay. The driver's mate was pinned beneath the roller and was killed.   *(courtesy R. Smith)*

67, 68, 69 & 70.   Aveling & Porter 7 ton Shay tandem steam roller No 7411 ■, Registration No XP 2915, was built in October 1912 and sold to Fulham Corporation, London. In 1928 she was sold to W.W. Buncombe of Highbridge, Somerset where she became No 118 in their fleet. The double cylinder engine was built under Ephraim Shay's American Patent of 1881 and was mounted on the right hand side of the vehicle and drove the rear axle by means of a bevel gear.   (courtesy N.D. Buncombe)

71.   An Aveling & Porter single cylinder steam roller after running away down a hill approaching Backwell on the Bristol to Weston-super-Mare road. Thought to be just after the First World War. *(courtesy N.D. Buncombe)*

72.   An Aveling & Porter compound steam roller fitted with Morrison's patent scarifier seen with a broken front fork after running away in Hill Street, Birmingham in 1919.   *(courtesy Road Roller Association)*

73 & 74. An Aveling & Porter steam roller, photographed by E.R. Passey of Blackwood, Monmouthshire, after an accident presumed to have happened in this area circa 1914. The roller ran away down a hill and the driver attempted to stop her by steering into the bank, whereupon she turned over. The two men posing with the roller seem to have assumed the air of heroes but the owners, Eddison Steam Rolling Company of Dorchester, no doubt viewed them in a different light. *(courtesy Eddison Plant Ltd)*

75. Aveling & Porter 6 ton single cylinder steam roller No 7828, Registration No FX 7006, was built in November 1912 and sold to Eddison Steam Rolling Company of Dorchester, Fleet No 199, where she spent all of her working life. In this photograph, dated 9th February 1951, she is fitted with a two tine Oxford scarifier No 297, rolling in foundations for the road widening scheme at Waterloo Station in preparation for the Festival of Britain traffic. The driver is Charlie Joyce.
(courtesy J.H. Meredith)

76. Aveling & Porter 10 ton single cylinder steam roller No 9078, Registration No HR 4398 was built in February 1920 and sold to Barnes Bros of Southwick, Wiltshire where she spent all of her working life. This photograph was taken in 1928 at Berkhamsted after an accident.
(courtesy J.W. Cole)

77. A pair of Aveling & Porter 8 ton single cylinder steam rollers photographed in the yard of Bertie J. Aldridge of Pulham St Mary, Norfolk in the mid 1960s. On the left is No 9155 ■, Registration No NO 2085, which was built in September 1920 and sold to C.J. Wills & Sons Ltd of Becontree Estate, Essex. She was sold to Thos. C. White of Guildford before being acquired by Aldridge by 1957. To the right is Class 'E' 10 ton single cylinder steam roller No 10235 ■, Registration No NO 4558, which was built in February 1922 and sold to C.H. Hawkins of Great Clacton, Essex.

(courtesy Bertie J. Aldridge & Sons Ltd)

78. Aveling & Porter 10 ton compound steam roller No 9186, Registration No CJ 4527, was built in July 1920 and sold to Hereford County Council becoming No 4 in their fleet. She spent all her working life with the council and is seen at work on 11th August 1953.

(courtesy R.G. Pratt)

79. Aveling & Porter 10 ton single cylinder steam roller No 9192, Registration No ER 1852, was built in August 1920 and sold to Cambridge County Council where she became Fleet No 1. She spent all of her working life with this owner before being sold in December 1951 to scrap dealer Richard Duce of Cambridge. This photograph was taken on the outskirts of Cambridge in 1949.

(courtesy R.G. Pratt)

80. Aveling & Porter 8 ton compound tandem steam roller No 9216, Registration No J 8752, was built in August 1920 and sold to Durham County Council. In 1924 she was sold to Eddison Steam Rolling Company of Dorchester where she became their Fleet No 563, they were the last recorded owners.

(courtesy F.H. Gillford)

81.   Aveling & Porter 10 ton single cylinder steam roller No 9399, Registration No AY 9518, was built in February 1921 and sold to Leicestershire County Council where she spent her working life as their Fleet No 27. This photograph was taken at Cosby, Leicestershire on 24th March 1950.

(courtesy R.E. Tustin)

82.   Aveling & Porter 10 ton type 'F' compound steam roller No 10058, Registration No DF 7254, was built in November 1921 and sold to Stroud Urban District Council. In 1932 she was sold to R Furborough & Sons of Wolvey, Warwickshire. Eventually she was acquired by T.J. Galliford & Sons also of Wolvey who were her last recorded owners. This photograph shows her after a mishap whilst owned by Stroud UDC, even in those days the broken piece of the headstock bearing the brass horse soon disappeared.

(author's collection)

83.   Aveling & Porter 8 ton Type 'D' steam roller No 10072 ∎, Registration No YA 3783, was built in April 1922 and sold to Bridgwater Rural District Council, later becoming the property of Somerset County Council being given their Fleet No 50. As a result of the accident shown in this photograph she was sold to W.W. Buncombe of Highbridge, Somerset in 1963 and replaced with a new Marshall diesel roller. She was overhauled by Buncombe's and sold to a contractor eventually finishing up in Four Water Children's Playing Ground at Cwmbran.

(courtesy N.D. Buncombe)

84. Aveling & Porter 10 ton Type 'E' single cylinder steam roller No 10159 ■, Registration No NO 3867, was built in July 1921 and sold to Leyton Urban District Council, Essex. By 1936 she had been sold to F.W. Cleare, Co of Burnham, Bucks, later going to Thomas T. Boughton & Son of Amersham Common.

(courtesy C. Roads)

85. Aveling & Porter Type 'O' Quick Reverse tandem steam roller believed to be No 10245, Registration No AT 6532, which was built in March 1922 and sold to Hull Corporation where she worked until 1937, when she was sold to John Dickinson & Son (Emley) Ltd. The following year she was acquired by James Carmichael of Lochgilphead, Argyllshire and in 1941 by Crowley Russell & Company of Airdrie, Scotland, who were her last recorded owners. This type of roller was introduced to meet the demand for a quick reversing machine capable of rolling bituminous carpet or tarmacadam surfacing. They were fitted with a vertical firetube boiler which supplied steam to the double high pressure cylinders. The driver sat over the rear roll facing the boiler with his right hand on the vertical steering wheel which controlled the steam steerage engine.

(courtesy Road Roller Association)

86.   Aveling & Porter 8 ton Type 'C' single cylinder steam roller No 10258, Registration No FX 8724, was built in 1922 and sold to Eddison Steam Rolling Company of Dorchester where she was given the Fleet No 376. The steam roller was cut up in 1962.

(courtesy Eddison Plant Ltd)

87 & 88.   Aveling & Porter 10 ton Type 'E' single cylinder steam roller No 10410, Registration No FX 9682, was built in October 1922 and sold to Eddison Steam Rolling Company of Dorchester where she spent all of her working life becoming No 416 in their fleet. These two photographs were taken on 30th July 1951 at Moor Row Railway Station (near Whitehaven), Cumberland when she went through the bridge and fell onto the tracks. The railway executive subsequently paid Eddison compensation for the failure of the bridge and presumably she was scrapped at this time.

(courtesy Eddison Plant Ltd)

89.   Aveling & Porter 8 ton Type 'C' single cylinder steam roller No 10421, Registration No FX 9723, was built in October 1922 and sold to the Eddison Steam Rolling Company of Dorchester where she spent all of her working life being No 421 in the fleet. In this photograph taken in Devon Road, Salcombe in May 1958 she has been breaking up the road surface with her Morrison scarifier in the course of re-shaping the carriageway for the Salcombe Urban District Council. The driver was P. Hibberd, with driver Critchell on the Drott Shovel (Registration No TO 1710) with foreman A. Lapthorne surveying the scene.

(courtesy Eddison Plant Ltd)

90.   Aveling & Porter 8 ton Type 'C' single cylinder steam roller No 10444, Registration No FX 9765, was built in November 1922 and sold to the Eddison Steam Rolling Company of Dorchester where she spent all her working life, becoming No 428 in their fleet.   *(courtesy Eddison Plant Ltd)*

91. Aveling & Porter 10 ton Type 'E' single cylinder steam roller No 10555 ■, Registration No YA 5591, was built in April 1923 and sold to W.W. Buncombe of Highbridge, Somerset where she was given the Fleet No 42. In March 1958 she was overhauled in Buncombe's works before being sold to Paignton Urban District Council. This photograph shows her just out of works awaiting delivery.
(courtesy N.D. Buncombe)

92. Aveling & Porter 6 ton Class 'B' compound steam roller No 10828, Registration No PR 2046, was built in February 1924 and sold to the Eddison Steam Roller Company of Dorchester where she became No 552 in their fleet and where she spent all of her working life being last licenced in 1955. This photograph was taken in June 1950.
(courtesy Ronald H. Clark)

93. Aveling & Porter 8 ton Type 'C' single cylinder steam roller No 10926 ■, Registration No AD 8772, was built in June 1924 and sold to Cirencester Urban District Council in Gloucestershire. She was later sold to R. Dingle & Sons of Stoke Climsland, Cornwall, where she spent her working life before eventually going into preservation.
(courtesy R. Dingle & Sons)

94. Aveling & Porter 6 ton Type 'B' compound steam roller No 10939, Registration No BB 9224, was built in June 1924 and sold to Newcastle-upon-Tyne Corporation where she spent all of her working life. In 1957 she was sold to Guy Potts of Harbottle, County Durham and scrapped. This photograph was taken in Glue House Lane on 30th December 1936 after involvement in a road accident.

(author's collection)

95. Aveling & Porter 6 ton Type 'B' compound steam roller No 10998, Registration No XU 4081, was built in July 1924 and sold to Lambeth Corporation, London where she stayed for all her working life. This photograph was taken in Lambeth Walk, on 27th July 1951.

(courtesy J.H. Meredith)

96. Aveling & Porter 8 ton Type 'C' single cylinder steam roller No 11671, Registration No PF 5351, was built in November 1926 and sold to G.S. Faulknor & Son of Reigate, Surrey. By December 1949 she was with Rowley Plant Hire Ltd and numbered No 19 in their fleet. By January 1958 she had been sold to R.J. Mitchell of Bromley, Kent who scrapped her the same year. This photograph was taken on Horse Guards Parade, London on 15th April 1954 and shows her at work scarifying.

(courtesy J.H. Meredith)

97.   Aveling & Porter 10 ton Type 'F' compound steam roller No 12156 ■, Registration No YW 4437, was built in May 1928 and sold to Wandsworth Corporation, London where she was No 6 in their fleet. By 1954 she had been sold to Arthur M. Cole of Sleaford, Lincolnshire. Her last owner before going into preservation was the Felixstowe Dock and Railway Company. This photograph was taken at Tooting Bec on the 22nd September 1951.   *(courtesy J.H. Meredith)*

98.   An Aveling & Porter 12 ton compound roller after an accident in the main street of St Ives, Cornwall in the summer of 1927. The roller was ascending the 1 in 5 hill out of the town when the driving pin came out of the rear wheel resulting in the roller and living van running backwards and jack-knifing across the road demolishing a shop front and trapping two small girls between the van and the roller's bunker, fortunately they escaped unhurt.   *(author's collection)*

99. Aveling & Porter 8 ton Type 'AC' single cylinder steam roller No 14113 ■, Registration No TM 8871, was built in May 1931 and sold to Bedford Corporation. In 1956 she was sold to C.A.E.C. Howard of Bedford but by 1958 had been acquired by G. Allen & Son of Luton. This photograph, taken in May 1964, shows her rolling the lorry park at John's Garage and Cafe, Girtford Bridge, Sandy, Bedfordshire.   *(Author)*

100. An unidentified Aveling & Porter steam roller at work on the London to Brighton Road in Surrey. A pitch macadam foundation with a bitumen carpet surface is being laid, both substances produced in a Ransome combined drying and mixing plant, the steam roller only being used to consolidate the foundations before the application of the dressings.   *(courtesy Road Roller Association)*

101. Burrell 10 ton single crank compound steam roller No 2145, Registration No BD 5618, was built in November 1898 and sold to J.J. Martin of Piddington, Northamptonshire. On a date not recorded she was sold to Esmond E. Kimbell of Boughton, Northants where she was last licenced in December 1952. This photograph shows her on the side of the A43 road near Stanion, Northants on 6th September 1952.

(courtesy G.H. Starmer)

102. Burrell 12½ ton single crank compound steam roller No 2338, was built in November 1900 and sold to S.T. Rosbotham of Bickerstaffe, Lancashire. By October 1908 she had been sold to Thomas Wood & Sons of Crockenhill, Kent, where she became No 10 in their fleet and eventually received the Registration No KK 2845. In 1930 she was converted into a traction engine for threshing although for some reason she never undertook this work before being scrapped in July 1946. This photograph from early in 1904 shows driver Jack Perrin, who was still driving her in 1926, and a road gang at work in Kent. *(courtesy Thomas Wood & Sons Ltd)*

103. Burrell 10 ton single crank compound steam roller No 2535, Registration No AH 6814, was built in November 1902 and sold to Thomas R. Doran (later Doran Bros) of Thetford, Norfolk where she spent all of her working life. *(courtesy R. Smith)*

104. Burrell 10 ton Class 'A' single crank compound steam roller No 2717 was built in December 1904 and sold to Henry Arden of Heavitree, Devon. In September 1905 she was sold to F. Sharp & Sons of Blandford, Dorset where she was given the Registration No FX 7207 and spent the rest of her working life being last licenced in December 1934. This photograph taken by W. Churchill of Wareham shows her after running through the side of a bridge near Wareham in 1906. *(courtesy R. Smith)*

105. Burrell 10 ton Class 'A' single crank compound steam roller No 2769 was built in August 1905 and sold to Fred Payne of Red Ball, Devon. In October 1907 she was sold to Doran Bros of Thetford, Norfolk where in due course she received the Registration No AH 6866 and spent the rest of her working life.

(courtesy R. Smith)

106. Burrell 10 ton double crank compound steam roller No 3047 ■, Registration No AH 6867, was built in October 1908 and sold to Thomas R. Doran of Thetford, Norfolk where she spent most of her working life. In 1960 she was sold to R. Palmer & Sons of West Dereham, Norfolk who sold her into preservation in 1962.

(courtesy R. Smith)

107 & 108.   Burrell 12 ton single crank compound steam roller No 3150, was built in October 1909 and sold to Winsby & Company, London for export. The photographs were taken outside the paint shop at the works on 11th October 1909.   *(author's collection)*

109 & 110.   Burrell 8 ton single cylinder steam roller No 3301, was built in May 1911 and sold to Samuel Jackson & Sons, Wistaston, Cheshire where she was given their Fleet No 14. In July 1918 she was sold to Eddison Steam Rolling Company of Dorchester where she became No 266 in their fleet and eventually received the Registration No FX 7052. In 1953 she was sold to scrap dealer J.W. Hardwick & Sons of West Ewell where she was cut up in the sixties. These are the official works photographs.   *(author's collection)*

111 & 112.   Burrell 10 ton Class 'A' compound steam roller No 3313 ■, Registration No AH 6813, was built in August 1911 and sold to Doran Bros of Thetford, Norfolk. At an unrecorded date she was sold to R. Palmer & Sons of West Dereham who eventually sold her into preservation. The top photograph shows the roller about to leave Doran Bros yard at Thetford with living van and water cart, and the driver and road gang pose against 3313 ■ in the lower photograph.   *(both courtesy R. Smith)*

113 & 114.   Burrell 6 ton compound steam roller No 3359, was built in September 1912 and sold to M. Saaf, Gothenburg, Sweden. She is seen in her official works photograph prior to shipment.   *(author's collection)*

115. Burrell 10 ton compound steam roller No 3364, Registration No MB 44, was built in February 1912 and sold to Wirral Rural District Council, later to become Cheshire County Council where she was given the Fleet No 20. In 1955 she was sold to Robert Bridson & Son of Neston, Cheshire where she spent the rest of her working life. This photograph shows her in Houton depot yard on 3rd November 1951.
(courtesy J.H. Meredith)

116 & 117. Burrell 5 ton steam wagon No 3760 which was bought by Edward J. Edwards of Norwich, Norfolk in 1923 where she received the Registration No CL 9237. In 1926 she was converted into a steam roller in which form she is seen working at Felixstowe on 19th June 1935.
(courtesy R.G. Pratt)

118.   Burrell 8 ton single crank cylinder steam roller No 3946 ■, Registration No YA 4521, was built in December 1922 and sold to William J. King of Bishop's Lydeard, Somerset where she spent her working life being sold into preservation in 1970.   *(courtesy R.E. Tustin)*

119.   Burrell 10 ton single crank compound steam roller No 4002, Registration No TD 653, was built in January 1925 and sold to S.T. Rosbotham of Bickerstaffe, Lancashire where she spent all of her working life. This works photograph shows her outside the paint shop prior to dispatch.   *(author's collection)*

120. Burrell 10 ton single cylinder steam roller No 4005 ■, Registration No RL 574, was built in March 1925 and sold to R. Dingle & Sons of Stoke Climsland, Cornwall, where she spent all of her working life until being sold into preservation in 1968. This is the official works photograph. *(author's collection)*

121. Burrell 8 ton compound steam roller No 4022, Registration No PU 7453, was built in April 1925 and sold to John Hardy of Blackmore, Essex, where she spent her working life. This photograph shows her at Northfleet on 13th January 1952. *(courtesy J.H. Meredith)*

122.　Burrell 10 ton Class 'A' compound steam roller No 4047, Registration No WU 8157, was built in July 1926 and sold to George E. Hall, of Shelley, West Riding of Yorkshire where she spent her working life. In 1961 she was sold to J. Summers of Grange Moor and scrapped. She is seen in her official works photograph.

(author's collection)

123.　Burrell 8 ton compound steam roller No 4052, Registration No TD 6990, was built in August 1926 and sold to John Ball of Forton, Lancashire, where she spent all of her working life. This photograph taken on 29th June 1954 shows her at work near Forton.　*(courtesy R.G. Pratt)*

124 & 125.   Burrell 8 ton single cylinder steam roller No 4058 ■, Registration No PX 5192, was built in November 1926 and sold to H. Kay Ltd, Horsham, West Sussex where she spent all of her working life before being sold into preservation.   *(author's collection)*

126. Burrell 8 ton single cylinder steam roller on the maker's stand at an agricultural show awaiting a purchaser.
(author's collection)

127. Burrell 8 ton compound steam roller No 4083 ■, Registration No RT 4058, was built in January 1928 and sold to Mutford & Lothingland Rural District Council which eventually became part of the East Suffolk County Council. This official works photograph shows her outside the paint shop prior to dispatch.
(author's collection)

128.   Clayton & Shuttleworth 12½ ton compound steam roller fitted with crane No 35350 was built in May 1903 and sold to the Admiralty for use in the dockyard at Chatham, Kent.   *(courtesy Ronald H. Clark)*

129.   Clayton & Shuttleworth 10 ton single cylinder steam roller No 44279, was built in December 1911 and sold to Mitchell & Speak of Halifax. She was sold to R. Cole Bros and received the Registration No CT 5124 whilst in their ownership but no other details are recorded. By August 1922 she had been sold to George Roberts & Sons of Caistor, Lindsay. In November 1942 she was purchased by T.W. Ward Ltd of Sheffield where she is seen in this photograph at work in the early forties for the Air Ministry.   *(courtesy P.G. Smart)*

130. Clayton & Shuttleworth 10 ton single cylinder steam roller No 48751 ■, Registration No YA 6182, was built in June 1923 and sold to W.W. Buncombe, Highbridge, Somerset where she spent all of her working life as their Fleet No 49, eventually being sold into preservation. This photograph was taken whilst she was working in West Suffolk but the date is not recorded.
(courtesy R.G. Pratt)

131. Clayton & Shuttleworth 10 ton single cylinder steam roller No 48792, Registration No YA 6979, was built in August 1923 and sold to W.W. Buncombe of Highbridge, Somerset where she spent all of her working life as No 70 in their fleet. She was last licenced in 1951. This photograph was taken in West Suffolk on an unknown date.
(courtesy R.G. Pratt)

132. Clayton & Shuttleworth ton single cylinder steam rolle No 49003, Registration No FF 2507, was built in May 1927 and sold to Davies Bros Barmouth, Merioneth where she spent all of her working life.   *(courtesy R.G. Pra*

133. Clayton Wagons Ltd built this 5 ton compound tandem steam roller No T1090 in January 1927 to the order of the India Office in London. Many of the features of their wagons were incorporated but only a small number were built and none appear to have survived.　　　　　　　*(courtesy Road Roller Association)*

134.　Foster 6 ton compound steam tractor No 13088 ■, Registration No FE 1140, was built in August 1913 and sold to E.E. Gwilt of Craven Arms, Salop. She was acquired by G.B. Davies & Sons of Ludlow who had sold her by 1921 to Staffordshire Haulage & Contracting Co Ltd of Wolverhampton where she received the Registration No AW 7327. Two further owners followed both in Staffordshire before she was sold to W.A. Bishop & Sons of Burley in 1947. They in turn sold her to R.M. Woolley of Bucknell who converted her into an 8 ton steam roller and where she received the Registration No FE 1125. By July 1960 she had been sold into preservation and is now back as a tractor. This photograph was taken at Bucknall in 1953.

(courtesy R.G. Pratt)

135. Fowler Class
'B' compound
road engine No
4614 was built in
1883 but fitted
with a front roll.
The reason for this
special
requirement and
the customer are
unfortunately not
recorded.
*(courtesy Institute of
Agricultural History)*

136. The first
Fowler steam
roller built in 1885
from a Class 'A'
compound traction
engine No 4839
which was sold
abroad.
*(courtesy Institute of
Agricultural History)*

137. Fowler 11 ton Class 'D' single cylinder steam roller No 6475 built in September 1891 and sold to the Lanchester Highway Board, County Durham after being displayed on Fowler's stand at the Royal Agricultural Society of England Show which was held at Doncaster in that year. Later she was sold to William Bland of Gosforth, Northumberland. Circa 1920 she was then sold to J. McLaren Junior of Gosforth where she received Registration No NL 1383. In 1932 she was sold to Northern Rollers Ltd of Birtley, County Durham where she spent the remainder of her working life. No date is given on the photograph which was taken in William Bland's ownership, and it is very likely that the owner and his son Steven, after whom the engine was named, also appear. *(author's collection)*

138. Fowler Class 'A3' single cylinder traction engine No 6754 was built in August 1892 and sold to Charles Parker of Headingley, Leeds. In July 1893 she was sold to Hampshire Bros of Mirfield, West Riding of Yorkshire and, at an unrecorded date, she was converted into a steam roller by T. Green & Sons Ltd of Leeds. She is seen at work in this photograph with the road gang. *(courtesy J. Hampshire)*

139.   Fowler 12 ton Class 'D2' single cylinder steam roller No 7943, Registration No E 5356 (later to become EE 5356), was built in November 1899 and sold to McLoughlin & Robinson of Stoke-on-Trent, Staffordshire. Later she was sold to John Allen & Sons (Oxford) Ltd which became John Allen & Ford Ltd. On the motion side cover she has a plate 'Ford & Son (Wokingham) Ltd'. She spent her working life with this company under its various titles until broken up by T.W. Ward for scrap in the late 1950s. This photograph shows her at work on the Oxford Bypass on 4th September 1955.   *(courtesy J.H. Meredith)*

140.   Fowler 10 ton single cylinder steam roller, works number not recorded, owned by Oxfordshire Steam Ploughing Company of Cowley, Oxford (afterwards to become John Allen & Sons (Oxford) Ltd). John Allen, the gentleman on the right, was not satisfied with the scarifiers available and in 1898 bought the patents of the Bomford scarifier for the sum of £300. This scarifier was a big advance on anything so far produced and was soon being made at the Cowley works. This photograph shows a demonstration of the new scarifier, possibly in Oxford.   *(courtesy Institute of Agricultural History)*

141.   Fowler 10 ton Class 'D2' single cylinder steam roller No 8593 was built in August 1900 and sold to Glamorgan County Council where she became No 5 in their fleet. By 1921 she had been sold to Oxford Steam Plough Company where she spent the rest of her working life as their Fleet No 52 and received the Registration No BW 4847. She was scrapped in 1949.   *(courtesy R.G. Pratt)*

142.   Fowler 10 ton Class 'DZ' single cylinder steam roller thought to be No 9008, Registration No FX 6915, was built in July 1901 and sold to Eddison & De Mattos Ltd (later the Eddison Steam Rolling Co Ltd, Dorchester) where she became No 84 in their fleet. She spent all of her working life with Eddison and was last licenced in 1946. This photograph shows her at work in Ashley Road, Parkstone in the care of driver S.B. Dodge, the second man is operating the Bomford scarifier.   *(courtesy Eddison Plant Ltd)*

143.   Fowler 15 ton Class 'A4' single cylinder steam roller No 9147, Registration No NL 1556, was built in March 1902 and sold to William Bland & Son of Gosforth, Northumberland. In 1957 she was sold to J.T. Lister & Sons of Consett, County Durham, probably for scrapping. In this photograph taken in 1912 she is seen working one of A.J. Henderson's patent independent scarifiers with rotating drills.

(courtesy Institute of Agricultural History)

144.   Official works photograph taken on 4th June 1903 of Fowler Class A5 compound spring mounted convertible steam roller No 9299 which was built in March 1903 for the War Office for service in Malta.

(author's collection)

145 & 146. Official works photographs of Fowler 12 ton single cylinder convertible steam roller No 9852 which was built in February 1904 and sold to Crook Urban District Council, County Durham. Upon a date not recorded but possibly circa 1920 she was sold to engine dealers James Graven of Ely, Cambridgeshire where she received the Registration No EB 4558. In 1924 she was sold to Plumbly & Gaze of North Walsham, Norfolk, where she was noted as being for sale in 1939.   *(courtesy Road Roller Association)*

147. Fowler Class 'E' three cylinder compound steam roller No 10105 was built in March 1905 and sold to the War Department for service in Gibraltar. In this photograph she is seen at Leeds demonstrating Fowler's independent scarifier before delivery. *(author's collection)*

148. Fowler 10 ton Class 'D2' compound steam roller No 10155, Registration No AW 9519 was built in March 1905 and sold to W. Edwards & Company, later Clee Hill Transport & Rolling Co Ltd where she became No 6 in their fleet and spent all of her working life, being last licenced in 1955. In this photograph she is seen at work at Clee Hill in May 1914. It is interesting to note the footpath which goes through the centre of the tree in the background. *(courtesy J.A. Smith)*

149.   Fowler 10 ton Class 'D2' compound steam roller No 10156, Registration No FJ 1531, was built in April 1905 and sold by their agent T.W. Letherton to Exeter Corporation (their Fleet No 1) where she was on show on his stand at the Devon Show in that year. In 1923 she was sold to W.W. Buncombe of Highbridge, Somerset where she spent the rest of her working life. This photograph shows her at the works prior to dispatch to Exeter.   *(courtesy Road Roller Association)*

150.   Fowler 10 ton Class 'D4' compound steam roller No 10808, Registration No WR 7884, was built in August 1910 and sold to Settle Rural District Council in the West Riding of Yorkshire. In 1951 she was sold to T.C. Potts of Great Harwood, Lancashire where she was scrapped in 1955. This official works photograph was taken on 4th August 1910.   *(courtesy Road Roller Association)*

151 & 152.   Fowler 12 ton Class 'D2' compound steam roller No 13457, Registration No E 5354, was built in November 1912 and sold to Stone Rural District Council in Staffordshire later to become Staffordshire County Council where she spent all of her working life. She was last licenced in December 1955. These photographs were taken on 9th July 1951 near Lichfield in Staffordshire.   *(courtesy P.N. Williams)*

153 & 154. Fowler 10 ton Class 'DN' single cylinder steam roller No 15589 ■, Registration No U 8709, was built in April 1921 and sold to David Wood & Company of Yeadon in the West Riding of Yorkshire where she spent her working life being sold into preservation by 1968. The upper photograph shows No 15589 ■ fitted with tar spraying equipment and rotary sweeping brush. The lower photograph shows her working with the Fowler-Wood patent tar-spraying and gritting machine. With this system a supplementary tank is fitted beneath the boiler to carry and heat the tar which is sprayed onto the road from jets mounted on the rear of the steam roller which are fed by a rotary pump chain-driven from the flywheel. The gritting machine which is coupled behind the steam roller spreads an even layer of stone chippings onto the hot coated road surface in a way far superior to hand spreading.   *(courtesy Institute of Agricultural History)*

155. Fowler Class
'DH1' 10 ton
single cylinder
steam roller
No 15942 ■,
Registration No
WY 8058, was
built in May 1923
and sold to
J.W. Stafford of
Clayton West (later
Hatfield), West
Riding of
Yorkshire where
she spent her
working life. This
official Fowler
photograph was
taken in 1928 at
Conisborough.
*(courtesy Institute of
Agricultural History)*

156. Official
works photograph
taken in 1930
illustrating a
Fowler steam
roller fitted with
the Fowler patent
'Invincible'
scarifier
implement
No 15247. This
photograph shows
the two tine size,
a three tine size
was also available.
*(courtesy Institute of
Agricultural History)*

157, 158 & 159. Fowler 10 ton Class 'D5' single cylinder steam roller No 16096, Registration No AT 8673, was built in March 1924 and sold to R. Dingle & Sons Ltd of Stokeclimsland, Cornwall where she spent all of her working life.

Fowler steam roller No 16096 photographed at work in June 1936.
(courtesy R.G. Pratt)

This photograph in 1931 shows driver Bert Oliver and his family who lived in the van pulled by the engine. If the driver was a good and capable man it was not unusual for his employer to let him have the use of an additional living van in which to bring up his family rather than lose him to a more static job.
(courtesy R. Dingle & Sons)

Fowler steam roller No 16096 and driver Bert Oliver pose with the road gang, circa 1931.
(courtesy R. Dingle & Sons)

160.   Fowler Class 'DH' 12 ton steam roller No 16272.   (courtesy Institute of Agricultural History)

161.   Another picture of Fowler Class 'DH' No 16272 was built in September 1925 and sold to Findlay Durham & Brodie the South African purchasing agents. This photograph taken at the works shows her in grey undercoat before returning to the paint shop to receive her finishing coats of paint. It is from the upstairs window of the building on the right that the photographer was able to get the picture on the opposite page looking down on her motion.   *(author's collection)*

162.   Fowler 10 ton class 'DN' single cylinder steam roller No 16615 ■, Registration No UM 3296, was built in December 1925 and sold to C.H. Johnson of Killingham in the West Riding of Yorkshire. In March 1931 she was sold to William Bland & Son of Gosforth, Northumberland. In 1950 she was sold to Gosforth Urban District Council who sold her into preservation in 1968. This photograph is reproduced from one of William Bland & Son's official postcards which they used for advertising purposes in the business.
(author's collection)

163.   Fowler Class 'DNB' 10 ton single cylinder steam roller No 18070 ■, Registration No YC 8375, was built in January 1929 and sold to W.J. King & Sons of Bishops Lydeard, Somerset where she spent her working life before being sold into preservation in 1970. In this photograph she is seen at work with W.J. King & Sons shortly after delivery.   *(courtesy Institute of Agicultural History)*

164.   Fowler 10 ton Class 'DNC' compound steam roller No 21833 ■, Registration No CRL 110, was built in 1936 and sold to R. Dingle & Sons of Stokeclimsland, Cornwall. In 1961 she was sold to Rowe & Company of Redruth before being sold into preservation in November 1963. This photograph shows her parked at the side of the Redruth Bypass on 25th March 1959.   *(courtesy G.H. Starmer)*

165.   Garrett 10 ton single cylinder steam roller No 21411 was built in 1898 and sold abroad. This is the official works photograph of the first steamroller built by the firm, the first for the English market being No 23377 built in June 1901.   *(courtesy R.G. Pratt)*

166.   Garrett No 4 Tractor No 27163 was built in 1908 and used as works tractor until October 1914 when she was sold to Henry Goult of Felixstowe, East Suffolk where she received the Registration No BJ 2314. By July she was in the ownership of Cocksedge & Co of Ipswich who sold her in 1936 to William Taylor of Sutterton, Lincs who converted her into a steam roller using Aveling front axle and rolls. In 1940 she was acquired by C.L. Bates of Bourne, Lincs where she worked until scrapped circa 1949. This photograph shows her at Gedney Railway Station on 19th October 1942.   *(courtesy Ronald H. Clark)*

167.   Garrett No 4 Type tractor No 33636 ■, Registration No BJ 4514, was built in September 1919 and sold to the Ecclesiastical Commissioners, Canterbury, Kent. She was later bought by W.C. Sutton & Sons of Beckermet, Cumberland who converted her into a steam roller in 1950. She was sold into preservation in 1973. This photograph was taken in Cumberland in August 1952.   *(courtesy R.G. Pratt)*

168.   Garrett 10 ton compound steam roller No 34084 ■, Registration No BJ 7045, was built in February 1922 and sold to East Suffolk County Council. At a later date she was sold to Sligo & Harrison of Lowestoft, East Suffolk and by August 1960 she had been acquired by Potter Bros of East Dereham, Norfolk where this photograph was taken in September of that year.   *(author's collection)*

169. Garrett 10 ton compound steam roller No 34085, Registration No BJ 7044, was built in February 1922 and sold to the East Suffolk County Council (South East Area) where she became No 5 in their fleet. She was sold to Sligo & Harrison of Lowestoft where she was scrapped in 1953.

(courtesy R.G. Pratt)

170. Garrett 10 ton compound steam roller No 34267 ■, Registration No BJ 9844, was built in October 1924 and sold to East Suffolk County Council where she became No 5 in their fleet. Her working life was spent with this owner until sold into preservation in 1969. She is seen in this photograph in a very undignified position after getting out of control on Swan Hill, Washbrook, Suffolk on 20th September 1937.

(courtesy R.G. Pratt)

171 & 172.   Two more pictures of Garrett No 34267 ■ after getting out of control at Swan Hill, Washbrook, Suffolk on 20th September 1937.

(courtesy R.G. Pratt)

173.   Garrett steam roller No 34267 ■ being towed away after the accident at Swan Hill, Washbrook, Suffolk on 20th September 1937.   *(courtesy R.G. Pratt)*

174.   Garrett 10 ton compound steam roller No 34706 ■, Registration No PU 7494, was built in March 1925 and sold to Z. Fairclough of Clacton-on-Sea, Essex. She was later acquired by A.M. Emeney of Hadleigh, West Suffolk and in 1953 became the property of J.T. Gray of Hadleigh who sold her for preservation in February 1964. This photograph was taken on the Old London Road at Capel St Mary, Ipswich whilst belonging to J.T. Gray.   *(courtesy R.G. Pratt)*

175.   Green 10 ton single cylinder steam roller (number unknown), Registration No CT 4352, was built in 1887 and sold to Thomas Cowman & Sons, Ashfordby, Leicestershire. It cannot be confirmed that they were the only or the original owners. This photograph was taken at Newstead Colliery, Nottinghamshire in 1925.

(courtesy F.H. Gillford)

176.   Green 10 ton single cylinder steam roller No 1374 was built in November 1889 and sold to Ilkeston Local Board, Derbyshire.

(courtesy F.H. Gillford)

177.   Green 8 ton single cylinder steam roller No 1430, Registration No TC 2386, was built in July 1898 and sold to Colne Borough Council, Lancashire. In August 1935 she went back to Thomas Green & Son Ltd presumably in part exchange as they scrapped her the same year.   *(courtesy W.P. Riley/B.D. Stoyel)*

178.   Green 8 ton single cylinder steam roller No 1505 was built in 1893 and sold to Otley Local Board, Yorkshire (Urban District Council from 1895). In August 1905 she was taken in part exchange by Aveling & Porter Ltd who sold her the same year to William Thackray & Sons, Old Malton, West Riding of Yorkshire where she received the Registration No AJ 6200 and spent the rest of her working life being last licenced in 1947. This photograph shows her awaiting her fate at Old Malton on 3rd October 1952.

(courtesy Ronald H. Clark)

179 & 180. Green 8 ton single cylinder steam roller No 1508 ■ was built in 1894 and sold to Derbyshire County Council where she became No 2 in their fleet. Circa 1919 she was sold to Hughes Bros of Chapel en le Frith, Derbyshire. These two photographs were taken in the late 1950s. *(Author)*

181.   Green 3 ton single cylinder steam roller No 1666, Registration No DN 2000, was built in August 1907 and sold to York Corporation where she spent her working life being last licenced in 1929. *(author's collection)*

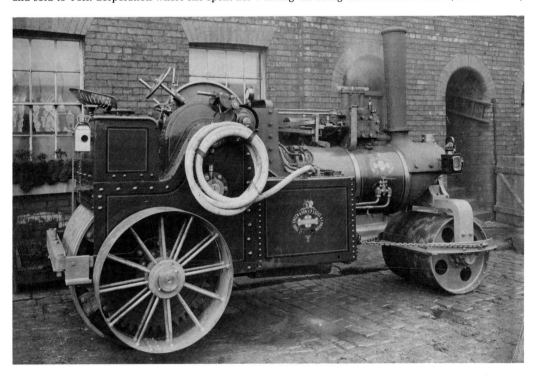

182.   Green single cylinder tandem steam roller of which no details are known. She appears to be new and her motion side cover plate has been removed for the photographer which would suggest that it is an official works photograph.   *(courtesy Ronald H. Clark)*

183. Green 10 ton single cylinder steam roller No 1976 was built in April 1918 for the War Department. In 1919 she was sold to Oxfordshire County Council where she received the Registration No BW 4949. In December 1927 she was acquired by engine and scrap dealer Geo Taylor of Redbourn, Hertfordshire where this photograph was taken on 22nd June 1936.

(courtesy R.G. Pratt)

184. Green 8 ton compound steam roller No 1995 was built in September 1919 for the War Department. Circa 1921 she was sold to Warwickshire County Council where she was given Fleet No 14 and received the Registration No AC 9305. By December 1923 she had been sold to Bower Bros of West Bridgford, Nottinghamshire. By 1949 she was with W.T. Palmer (Leicester) Ltd where this photograph was taken on 26th April 1949 at their Thurmaston Depot.

(courtesy R.E. Tustin)

185.   Green 10 ton single cylinder steam roller No 2007 ■, Registration No U 8432, was built in May 1920 and sold to Leeds Corporation where she spent her working life as their Fleet No 7. Eventually she was sold to scrap dealers J.W. Hinchcliffe Ltd of Leeds who sold her into preservation in 1965. This photograph shows her at Kirkstall Road Leeds in 1964.   *(courtesy D.A. Rayner)*

186.   Green 10 ton compound steam roller No 2201, Registration No WV 3254, was built in October 1925 and sold to Wakefield Rural District Council. In April 1930 she became the property of West Riding County Council Yorkshire and received their Fleet No 46. In 1955 she was sold to scrap dealer E. Sheard of Wakefield. In this photograph she is seen working at Mirfield, Yorkshire in June 1948.   *(courtesy J.A. Smith)*

187.   Green 10 ton compound steam roller No 2408, Registration No RY 5047, was built in July 1927 and sold to Smith & Hutchinson Ltd of Leicester. In 1932 she was sold to F.W. Clarke of Leicester and finally to W.T. Palmer (Leicester) Ltd of Thurmaston, Leicestershire where she was last licenced in 1952.

(courtesy P.G. Smart)

188.   A Green 10 ton tandem compound steam roller lying derelict in the yard of Palmers of West Dereham, Norfolk. Unfortunately there are no further details of this rare and very interesting roller.

(courtesy Ronald H. Clarke)

189 & 190.   McLaren 10 ton single cylinder convertible steam roller No 284, Registration No HD 1577, was built in August 1887 and sold to Hampshire Bros of Ravensthorpe, Dewsbury, Yorkshire where she spent all of her working life. In the above photograph she is seen circa 1910 in the Woollen district and below in their yard around the same date. Tom Hampshire is in front of the rear roll in both photographs.

(courtesy J. Hampshire)

(courtesy R.G. Pratt)

191 & 192.   McLaren 10 ton compound steam roller No 1694, Registration No MO 1854, was built in June 1923 and sold to Newbury Rural District Council, Berkshire, eventually being acquired by Berkshire County Council. In 1933 she was sold to Ford & Son of Wokingham, where she worked for the rest of her life being last licenced in 1952.

(courtesy C. Roads)

193.   Another view of McLaren No 1694 at work when in the ownership of T. Ford & Son, of Wokingham, Berkshire.   *(courtesy C. Roads)*

194.   McLaren 10 ton compound steam roller No 1702, Registration No WT 1693, was built in January 1924 and sold to Bowland Rural District Council in the West Riding of Yorkshire. She spent her working life with this authority until sold in 1956 to Sutcliffe Bros of Todmorden for scrapping. *(courtesy Road Roller Association)*

195 & 196. Manning Wardle 15 ton double cylinder steam roller built circa 1865 to the French Ballaison-Gellerat design. How many of this design were built at Leeds is not recorded but it is fairly certain that only this one example was made and there is no record of it being in commercial use.

(courtesy Institute of Agricultural History)

197.   Mann's light steam roller for rolling tarmacadam or water bound materials. The tank over the rear roll carried water for the sprinklers. The weight of the roller could be varied by the amount of water carried. This photograph is taken from Mann's catalogue and no other details are recorded.   *(courtesy Ronald H. Clark)*

198.   Mann's 6¼ ton patching steam roller, works number not recorded, Registration No DX 3028, believed to have been supplied new to Ipswich Corporation. Later sold to Edward J. Edwards of Norwich where she is seen in this photograph after having run away down Ketts Hill, Norwich.   *(courtesy R.G. Pratt)*

199.   Marshall 10 ton compound steam roller No 40047 ■, Registration No BE 8186, was built in March 1904 and sold to Gainsborough Rural District Council, Lincolnshire where she became No 4 in their fleet. Later she became the property of Lindsey County Council who eventually sold her into preservation. This photograph shows her at Brigg on 24th August 1955.   *(courtesy R.G. Pratt)*

200.   Marshall 6 ton convertible steam tractor No 72096 ■, Registration No BE 5066, built in November 1919 and sold to Mornement & Ray of East Harling, Norfolk who used her as a steam roller from July 1925. This photograph was taken at East Harling on 3rd August 1947.   *(courtesy R.G. Pratt)*

201. Marshall 6 ton convertible compound steam roller No 73821, Registration No AH 2383, was built in January 1921 and sold to Blofield & Flegg Rural District Council, Norfolk. In 1930 she was sold to May Gurney & Co Ltd, Trowse, Norwich, where she worked until scrapped in 1950. This photograph was taken at Trowse on 19th August 1936.   *(courtesy R.G. Pratt)*

202. Marshall 10 ton compound steam roller No 76634, Registration No TC 4179, was built in June 1923 and sold to Burnley Rural District Council which was later to be absorbed into Lancashire County Council. In 1952 she was sold to Todd Bros (St Helens & Widnes) Ltd where she was finally scrapped.

(author's collection)

(courtesy
Marshall Sons & Co Ltd)

203 & 204.
Two works
photographs of the
Millars-Marshall
double-cylinder
tandem steam
roller. The upper
illustration is
possibly the first
of the class
No 76945,
Registration No
TS 4231, built in
September 1923
and sold to the
Burgh of Dundee.
These rollers were
introduced
expressly to roll
tarmacadam,
asphalt,
bituminous and
other similar
materials that were
coming into use
for roadworks in
the early 1920s.

(courtesy
Road Roller Association)

205, 206 & 207.
An unknown Marshall tandem steam roller. This machine was built with a horizontal boiler as many customers disliked the vertical boiler. It was not a success so it would seem that customer resistance was as much against the tandem design as the vertical boiler.

(courtesy Ronald H. Clark)

208.   Marshall 10 ton single cylinder 'S' Type steam roller No 78667 ■, Registration No HO 6360, was built in February 1925 and sold to E.W. Wright of Alton, Hampshire. Her next owner was E.E. Kimbell of Boughton, Northamptonshire, although the date he acquired her is not known. She spent the rest of her working life with him until being sold into preservation in 1964. This photograph shows her at Boughton on 17th November 1952.

(courtesy R.G. Pratt)

209.   Marshall 6 ton convertible compound steam roller No 78928, Registration No SB 2285, was built in April 1925 and sold to Kenneth McRae & Sons, Oban, Argyll. Upon a date not recorded she was sold to William Tawse Ltd of Aberdeen where she spent the rest of her working life as their Fleet No 10. This photograph shows her by Loch Ness in 1937.

(courtesy R.G. Pratt)

210. Marshall 8 ton compound steam roller No 78953 ■, Registration No TD 2652, was built in July 1925 and sold to Huyton with Roby Urban District Council, Lancashire. She had two further owners before being sold into preservation, Joshua Rodgers of South Crosland, West Riding of Yorkshire and Isaac Timmins Ltd of Dalton. This photograph was taken at South Crosland in July 1950. *(courtesy J.A. Smith)*

211. Marshall 10 ton single cylinder steam roller No 79087 ■, Registration No NR 6120, was built in April 1925 and sold to Market Harborough Rural District Council. Later she became the property of the Leicestershire County Council Highways Committee and was sold for preservation in the early 1960s. This photograph was taken in the depot at Foxton Turn on 22nd April 1960. *(courtesy G.H. Starmer)*

212 & 213.   Two works photographs of a Marshall 10 ton 'Universal' double cylinder steam roller thought to be No 79444 ■, which was built in June 1925 and exhibited at the Transport Exhibition in London that year. She returned to the works and came out as No 80224 ■, Registration No MO 7021 with a building date recorded as March 1926. She was then sold to Ford & Son (Wokingham) Ltd, Berkshire where she became No 4 in their fleet. Later she was acquired by the War Department and used by the Royal Engineers at Liphook. She was later acquired for preservation.   *(courtesy Ronald H. Clark)*

214. Marshall 8 ton compound steam roller No 80730, Registration No WB 4857, was built in February 1926 and sold to John E. Nadin & Son, Sheffield & Liverpool where she became No 1 in their fleet and spent all of her working life. This photograph was taken in Sheffield in August 1953.   *(courtesy J.H. Meredith)*

215. Marshall 10 ton compound steam roller No 84620 ■, Registration No WF 2388, was built in May 1929 and sold to Cottingham Urban District Council, East Riding of Yorkshire and later she became the property of Haltemprice Urban District Council, in the East Riding. In 1964 she was sold into preservation. This photograph was taken at Hessle on 28th July 1951.   *(courtesy P.N. Williams)*

(courtesy Road Roller Association)

216 & 217.   Marshall embankment steam roller No 86990 was built in June 1933 for the Durham County Water Board. Two others were built in 1938, No 8268 for the South Essex Water Works Company of Abberton and No 88301 for the Corby & District Water Company of Market Harborough, Leicestershire. These were made for consolidating the banks of reservoirs. They had Sentinel vertical boilers and high speed duplex Marshall horizontal engines.

(courtesy Marshall Sons & Co Ltd)

218. Marshall 10 ton double cylinder tandem roller No 87125 ■, Registration No VG 5718, was built in July 1933 and sold to Norwich Corporation and became No 8 in their fleet. By 1946 she had been sold to Ben Jordan of Coltishall, Norfolk who in turn sold her to G.T. Cushing of Thursford although the date is not recorded. By September 1960 she was owned by Potter Bros of East Dereham later being sold into preservation. This photograph shows her at Thursford in August 1954.

(courtesy R.G. Pratt)

219. Marshall 10 ton 'Universal' double cylinder steam roller No 87635 ■, Registration No APX 542, was built in June 1935 and sold to West Sussex County Council where she became No 49 in their fleet and where she spent her working life being sold into preservation in 1964. This photograph was taken at Drayton, near Chichester, Sussex on 11th September 1963.

(courtesy J.H. Meredith)

220. A Ransomes Sims & Jefferies convertible steam roller thought to be No 11829, built in May 1898. Very few of these convertibles were built and the firm did not involve itself with the steam roller market.

(author's collection)

221. Official photograph of Robey 7 ton compound tandem steam roller No 40651, Registration No FE 4924, built in August 1922 and sold to Lincoln Corporation where she became No 4 in their fleet, and where she spent all of her working life.

(courtesy Road Roller Association)

222. Robey 7 ton compound tandem steam roller No 41609, Registration No OI 6916, was built in September 1924 and sold to Belfast Corporation where she became No 7 in their fleet and where she spent all of her working life. This photograph shows her at work outside the City Hall in June 1947.

(courtesy R.G. Pratt)

223. Official works photograph of Robey 8 ton compound tandem steam roller No 42156, Registration No FE 6535, built in December 1924 and sold to William Briggs & Sons Ltd of Dundee where she spent all of her working life and was last licenced in 1951.

(courtesy Ronald H. Clark)

224 & 225. Robey 7 ton compound tandem steam roller No 44083 ■, Registration No VL 2370, was built in May 1930 and sold to Wirksworth Quarries Ltd of London N1. In January 1935 she was acquired by Inns & Co Ltd of Woolmer Green, Hertfordshire who then traded as Wirksworth Quarries. During their ownership she was converted into a tri-tandem roller and spent the rest of her working life with the company until sold into preservation in 1964. In the top photograph 44083 ■ is seen in her tandem state at work in Berkhamsted High Street in 1934 and below as converted to a tri-tandem roller at work on the Watford by-pass in 1948. In both of these photographs her driver is the late Fred Barker.

(both author's collection)

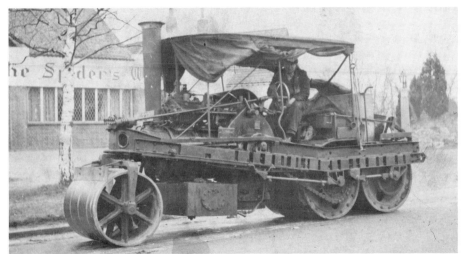

226.   Robey 6 ton compound tandem steam roller No 46935 ■, Registration No CZ 2432, was built in May 1933 and sold to Belfast Corporation where she became No 9 in their fleet. Towards the end of her working life she was sold to T. Spence of Moira, County Down from where she was sold into preservation. Photographed in Belfast in June 1947.   *(courtesy R.G. Pratt)*

227.   Robey 8 ton compound tandem steam roller No 48869 ■, Registration No EDV 916, was built in March 1939 and sold to Devon County Council (Northern Division) where she received the Fleet No 171, and later, presumably upon reorganisation, she received the number 116. She spent all of her working life with the council until sold into preservation in 1957.   *(courtesy Road Roller Association)*

228.   Ruston Proctor 15 ton single cylinder steam roller No 26620 was built in March 1903 and sold to East Retford Borough Council, Nottinghamshire. Her next owners were Cole Bros of Roxholme and then engine dealers George Thurlow & Sons of Stowmarket who presumably took her in part exchange against another roller. In 1918 they sold her to William J. King of Bishops Lydeard, Somerset where she received the Registration No YA 1769. In 1921 he sold her to R. & J. Kent of Baughurst, Hants. By 1940 she was with A. Streeter & Company of Godalming, Surrey, her last recorded owner. This photograph shows her in the ownership of R. & J. Kent.   *(courtesy C. Roads)*

229.   An unknown Ruston Proctor 12½ ton Class 'SR' single cylinder steam roller built circa 1907 and fitted with a Ruston 3 tine patent reversible scarifier.   *(courtesy R.E. Hooley)*

230.   An unknown Ruston Proctor Class 'SCR' compound steam roller seen on the stand of their Canadian agents, Mussens Ltd of Toronto, at the Toronto Exhibition in 1912.   *(courtesy R.E. Hooley)*

231.   Ruston Proctor 11 ton single cylinder steam roller No 43831, Registration No BJ 6013, was built in March 1912 and sold to Alfred Dawson, Rushmere St Andrew, East Suffolk where she became No 3 in his fleet and spent all her working life and is noted as still being in his ownership in 1944. The date of this professionally taken photograph is not recorded but a note on the back says 'He left his bicycle in view in the hedge'.   *(courtesy R.G. Pratt)*

232. Ruston Proctor 11 ton single cylinder steam roller No 43833, Registration No BJ 6014, was built in March 1912 and sold to Alfred Dawson of Rushmere St Andrew, East Suffolk where she became No 5 in his fleet and spent all of her working life. This undated photograph shows Alfred Dawson with one of his road gangs.   *(courtesy Road Roller Association)*

233. Ruston & Hornsby 10 ton single cylinder steam roller No 52785 ■, was built in January 1920 for the War Department. Later that year she was sold to the West Riding County Council where she became No 5 in their fleet and received the Registration No WR 6808. By 1966 she had been sold into preservation. This photograph was taken in the mid-twenties and shows her at work in Rigg Lane, Garforth under the care of driver Frank Horsley.   *(courtesy Miss M. Spinks)*

234. Ruston & Hornsby 11 ton compound steam roller No 112562, Registration No AY 9520, was built in May 1920 and sold to Leicestershire County Council. By August 1951 she had been sold to Jelson Ltd of Leicester. Photographed at Anstey on 1st July 1953.
(courtesy R.E. Tustin)

235 & 236. A Ruston & Hornsby single cylinder Class 'SR' steam roller thought to be the prototype machine No 157574, Registration No PG 3342, built in October 1929 and sold to Franks, Harris Bros Ltd of Guildford, Surrey where she spent all of her working life and was last licenced in 1953. Very few of this type or of the compound type 'SCR' were built but it was to become the Aveling standard design in the second half of the thirties when Rustons rescued them from the financial collapse of the A.G.E. Group of which they were members.
(courtesy R.G. Pratt)

237. Tasker Class 'A2' single cylinder convertible tractor No 1715 ■, was built in January 1917 for the War Department. Circa 1920 she was sold to H. Kay of Horsham, West Sussex where she was used in the roller configuration and received the Registration No BP 6289. In 1955 she was sold into preservation. This photograph shows her at work at Friston in 1937. *(courtesy R.G. Pratt)*

238. Tasker compound tandem steam roller No 1913, was built in 1924 to an order from Kirkcudbright County Council, Scotland but subsequently cancelled. She was not sold until June 1931 when she went to A.E. Prior of Limehouse, London her last recorded owner. She was the only tandem roller built by Taskers and bearing in mind the initial cancellation and the seven years in stock it would appear that the design did not meet with approval. Both tractor and wagon components were used in her construction.

(courtesy Ronald H. Clark)

239. A Wallis & Steevens 10 ton single cylinder steam roller belonging to W.W. Buncombe of Highbridge, Somerset seen at work at East Callow, Wantage in Berkshire. The crew are on the left, the driver was a man named Mercer Lee and the sweeper was Cooky Wiltshire. The imposing looking man with watch and chain was the Wantage Urban District Council's foreman with one of his men.
(courtesy N.D. Buncombe)

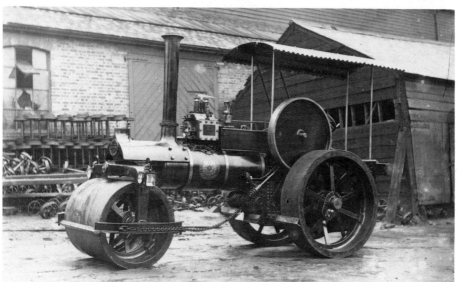

240. Official works photograph of Wallis & Steevens 8 ton single cylinder steam roller No 2539 which was built in November 1900 and sold to the Crown Agents for the Selangor Public Works Department in the State of the Malay Peninsula.
(courtesy P.G. Smart)

241. Wallis & Steevens 10 ton steam roller No 2556, Registration No HO 5833, was built in June 1901 and sold to the City of Winchester. In 1930 she was presumably taken in part exchange by Aveling & Porter Ltd who sold her in the same year to Mark Loader & Sons of Winton, Bournemouth where she was last licenced in 1941. This photograph was taken in the works yard prior to delivery.
(courtesy P.G. Smart)

242. Wallis & Steevens 10 ton single cylinder steam roller No 2572, was built in April 1902 and sold to William Lodge & Company of Shepton Mallet, Somerset. Circa 1912 she was sold to the Eddison Steam Rolling Company of Dorchester where she became No 197 in their fleet later receiving the Registration No FX 7004. Her last recorded owner was the firm of Matthew & Wood of Newport, Monmouthshire. This photograph circa 1913 was taken three miles from Ledbury after running through the side of a bridge due to an alleged fault in the steering gear. The man standing with his hand on top of the boiler is Bob Foster the boiler maker sent from Dorchester to recover the roller. *(courtesy Eddison Plant Ltd)*

243. Wallis & Steevens 3½ ton single cylinder steam roller No 2813 was built in March 1907 for the Crown Agents for Southern Nigeria. This photograph shows her in the station yard prior to dispatch.

(author's collection)

244. Wallis & Steevens 6 ton single cylinder steam roller No 2816 was built in January 1907 for James Pollock & Sons Co Ltd for shipment to Penang in the Straits Settlements. Official photograph taken in the station yard prior to dispatch.
(author's collection)

245. Wallis & Steevens 4¼ ton compound steam roller No 2889, Registration No AA 2106, was built in April 1906 and sold to Sheppard Bros. Ltd, Newport, Isle of Wight, where she spent all of her working life. This photograph was taken in the London & South Western Railway goods yard at Basingstoke when she was new.
(author's collection)

246. Official works photograph of Wallis & Steevens 6 ton compound oil bath steam roller No 2978, built in April 1907 and sold to Selig Sonnenthal & Company Engineers for use overseas.
(author's collection)

247. Wallis & Steevens 10 ton single cylinder steam roller No 7070 was built in January 1909 and sold to W.W. Buncombe of Highbridge, Somerset. Circa 1913 she was sold to the Eddison Steam Rolling Company of Dorchester where she became No 209 in their fleet later receiving the Registration No FX 7015. This photograph shows her in Abingdon Street, Burnham on Sea being driven by the father of W.W. Buncombe.

(courtesy N.D. Buncombe)

248. Wallis & Steevens 10 ton single cylinder steam roller No 7128, Registration No PC 9170, was built in January 1911 and sold to Herbert Ward & Sons of Egham, Surrey where she spent all of her working life. In December 1954 she was sold to scrap dealer J.W. Hardwick & Sons of West Ewell, Surrey. In this photograph she is on hire to Parr Head & Clements Knowling Ltd where she is seen working at Rye House Electricity Generating Station on 23rd March 1952.

(courtesy J.H. Meredith)

249. Wallis & Steevens 15 ton compound steam roller No 7234, was built in January 1911 for Morgan & Elliott, the English representatives for the customer in Barcelona, Spain.
(author's collection)

250. Wallis & Steevens 10 ton single cylinder steam roller No 7715, Registration No DG 1831, was built in December 1921 and sold to Chipping Sodbury Rural District Council and later became the property of Gloucestershire County Council where she spent the rest of her working life. She is recorded as still being in their ownership in 1958. In this official works photograph she is painted grey all over as the finished print was required for use in their catalogue.
(author's collection)

251. Official works photograph of Wallis & Steevens 8 ton compound steam roller No 7723, built in April 1921 and sold to the High Commissioner for the Union of South Africa.
(author's collection)

252. Wallis & Steevens 8 ton single cylinder steam roller No 7737 was built in July 1921 and sold to B. Holland & Company for export to Rangoon, Burma.

(author's collection)

253. Wallis & Steevens 6 ton Advance type double cylinder steam roller No 7772, Registration No HO 6167, was built in 1923. This was the prototype Advance roller and was originally used as a demonstrator. In June 1924 she was re-registered becoming HO 6324 and was sold to John Douglas of Southampton. In 1929 she was returned to Wallis & Steevens possibly in part exchange. During 1930 and 1931 she was hired out and on 28th April 1931 was sold to Caroline M. Newitt of Princes Risborough, Buckinghamshire, her last recorded owner.

(courtesy P.G. Smart)

254. Official works photograph of Wallis & Steevens 8 ton compound steam roller No 7776, Registration No MF 2181, built in September 1923 and sold to R.H. Powis of Wembley, Middlesex. On a date not recorded she was sold to John Allen & Sons Ltd, Oxford where she was last licenced in 1942.

(courtesy P.G. Smart)

255. Wallis & Steevens 8 ton Advance type double cylinder steam roller No 7785, Registration No OR 3539, was built in March 1924 and sold to Willesden Urban District Council, Middlesex, where she was given the Fleet No 6 and spent all of her working life. This photograph was taken in Willesden in September 1952.
(courtesy J.H. Meredith)

256. Official works photograph of Wallis & Steevens 10 ton compound steam roller No 7797, Registration No CA 6658, built in May 1924 and sold to Colwyn Bay & Colwyn Urban District Council where she spent all of her working life. After 1953 she was sold to W. Simpson & Son Ltd of Llandudno who presumably scrapped her.

(author's collection)

257. Wallis & Steevens 10 ton compound steam roller No 7799 ■, Registration No HO 6354, was built in November 1924 and sold to R. & J. Kent of Baughurst, Hants where she spent her working life. She was sold into preservation circa 1964. In this picture she is seen painted grey for her official photograph.

(author's collection)

258. Official works photograph of Wallis & Steevens 3 ton Simplicity type single cylinder steam roller No 7832 ■, Registration No HO 6472, built in January 1926 and sold to E. Parry & Company of Putney, London becoming No 8 in their fleet. In April 1933 she was sold to W. & J. Glossop of Hipperholme, West Riding of Yorkshire where she worked until being sold into preservation circa 1959.
(courtesy Road Roller Association)

259. Wallis & Steevens 8 ton Advance type double cylinder steam roller No 7837, Registration No HO 6409, was built in May 1925 and sold to George Ewen, Petersfield, Hants. She was last licenced in 1956 when she was sold to E.W. Edney of Horndean. In 1960 she was scrapped by Hatley of Chandlers Ford, presumably as she required heavy boiler or firebox repairs which in those days were not considered financially viable. This photograph was taken on the A3 Portsmouth Road south of Petersfield on 13th June 1953.
(courtesy J.H. Meredith)

260. Wallis & Steevens 8 ton Advance type double cylinder steam roller No 7863 ■, Registration No HO 6495, was built in March 1926 and sold to the Limmer & Trinidad Lake Asphalt Co Ltd of Glasgow. In 1927 she was taken back by Wallis & Steevens presumably in part exchange as they sold her on 25th September to Three Hills Sand & Gravel Company of Codicote, Hertfordshire. Eventually she was acquired by Wirksworth Quarries Ltd (Inns & Co Ltd) of Woolmer Green, Hertfordshire. By April 1966 she had been sold into preservation.
(courtesy P.G. Smart)

261. Wallis & Steevens 10 ton Advance type double cylinder steam roller No 7878 ■, Registration No HO 6482, was built in February 1926 and sold to Torquay Borough Council, Devon, where she spent the whole of her working life before being sold into preservation in 1967. This photograph shows her at work on a 1 in 7 hill in Torquay.
(courtesy Road Roller Association)

262. Wallis & Steevens 10 ton Advance type double cylinder steam roller No 7884 ■, Registration No OT 927, was built in April 1926 and sold to Tarmac Ltd, Ettingshall, Staffordshire where she became No 6 in their fleet. By December 1936 she had been acquired by Wrights (Acton) Ltd of Hampshire where she was last licenced in 1951. After a further change of ownership she was sold to scrap dealers J.W. Hardwick & Sons of West Ewell where she languished until sold for preservation in 1980.   *(courtesy P.G. Smart)*

263. Wallis & Steevens 6 ton Advance type double cylinder steam roller No 7903, Registration No KM 8319, was built in November 1926 and sold to Bexley Urban District Council, Kent. In 1939 she was sold to C.W. Lambert of Horsmonden, Kent. She then had two further owners, Kings & Co Ltd of Glasgow, and O.L. Davies of Briton Ferry, Glamorgan where she was noted for sale in 1947. By July 1956 she had been sold to Maberly Parker Ltd of Taffswell, Glamorgan and finally scrapped in 1959.   *(courtesy C. Roads)*

264 & 265.   Wallis & Steevens 3 ton Simplicity type single cylinder steam roller No 7937 was built in July 1927 to the order of the Crown Agents for export to Nigeria. Quoting from the makers catalogue of the day, 'Simplicity is the keynote of the design, the aim in view having been to introduce a roller which can be safely handled by unskilled labour, and which will give the minimum of trouble in outlying districts. The relatively long fire grate permits the use of either coal of inferior quality or of wood; the water tank is of sufficient capacity for approximately a full day's work; highly paid skilled labour is not essential'. These photographs were taken at Basingstoke Railway goods yard when the roller was new.   *(author's collection)*